STOLEN

SMALL-GROUP BIBLE STUDY

CHRIS AND KERRY SHOOK

Small-Group experience written by BARRY CRAM

Published by LifeWay Press®

ISBN: 978-1-4158-7197-3
Item: 005469706

Dewey Decimal Classification: 248.84
Subject Headings: CHRISTIAN LIFE \ BLESSINGS \ GOD

To order additional copies of this resource,
order online at www.lifeway.com; write LifeWay Small Groups;
One LifeWay Plaza; Nashville, TN 37234-0175;
fax order to (615) 251-5933; or call toll-free (800) 458-2772.

Printed in the United States of America

Leadership and Adult Publishing
LifeWay Church Resources
One LifeWay Plaza
Nashville, TN 37234-0175

CONTENTS

ABOUT THE AUTHORS

Kerry and Chris Shook founded Woodlands Church, formerly Fellowship of The Woodlands, in 1993. Since then the church has grown to 17,000 in average attendance each weekend. It is one of the fastest-growing churches in America.

Kerry is the senior pastor of Woodlands Church. He is one of today's most gifted communicators offering a clear, contemporary, and creative teaching style. Kerry strives to eliminate the barriers of boredom, unfriendliness, and fear that keep people from experiencing a relationship with Jesus Christ.

Chris is the Director of Missions and Women's Ministry at Woodlands Church. Her missions work has touched thousands of under-resourced people locally and in numerous countries around the world. Her women's ministry is one of the largest in the country providing fellowship, worship, and Bible study opportunities to hundreds of women each week.

Kerry and Chris wrote the New York Times best-seller *One Month to Live: Thirty Days to a No-Regrets Life* as well as *Love at Last Sight: Thirty Days to Grow and Deepen Your Closest Relationships.*

Kerry and Chris have been married over 25 years and have four children.

A WORD FROM THE AUTHORS

We go to great lengths to protect the things that mean the most to us. We secure our homes to feel safe and deposit our monies in trusted banks. Yet all the while an unseen thief is stealing the most valuable treasures we possess—our joy, our peace of mind, our courage, our purpose, and our relationships. Before long, we begin to settle for so much less than God intended for us and accept that as normal.

Chris and I experienced this all too often until we discovered what was really happening and how we could reclaim those stolen treasures. *Stolen* shares our own journey and points you to the evidence from God's Word that will awaken you to the treasure the enemy has stolen and how you can reclaim what is rightly yours.

God offers each of us a rich inheritance. It's our prayer that you will possess and enjoy all the riches that are yours in Christ.

Blessings,
Chris and Kerry Shook

SESSION 1

STOLEN INHERITANCE

Albert Einstein once said, "The value of a man resides in what he gives and not in what he is capable of receiving." But why is it that "not receiving" has a more virtuous value than "gaining or receiving"?

If we begin with humanity at the center of our realities, then finding value in selfless living may fit our worldview. It is noble to sacrifice. But if we begin with God—His plan and His values—we may come to a very different conclusion. God gave us something so inherently valuable that the Enemy will try every trick in his book to steal it from us.

Consider this: Instead of believing that we need to give, give, give to find our value in God's eyes, why not pursue the notion that we should take back what is rightfully ours? Recapture that which was intended from the beginning. Our inheritance. Our original glory. Our intrinsic worth.

FLASHBACK

*10 minutes

Use this time to talk as a group about what you hope to gain from this study.

What is it about reclaiming the treasures God intended for you—the things Satan has stolen—that most appeals to you?

What are your expectations of this study?

FRAMING THE STORY

*5-10 minutes

Why do you think leaving an inheritance is important?

How would you define the word *inheritance*?

Watch video session 1: "Stolen Inheritance" (17:50).

REEL TIME

*10 minutes

Fill in the blanks below on important points as you view the message from Kerry and Chris. You'll unpack this information with the group after the video.

Satan wants to:

steal your ____joy____,

kill your ____dreams____,

and destroy your ____relationships____.

When you commit your life to Christ, you ____inherit____ all that comes with being a son or daughter of the King.

Satan tries to cover up the ____evidence____ of your inheritance.

We are complete in Christ; we lack ____nothing____.

The evidence of your value is already complete in ____Christ____.

JOHN 10:10

"A thief comes only to steal and to kill and to destroy. I have come so that they may have life and have it in abundance."

COLOSSIANS 2:9-10 (NIV)

For in Christ all the fullness of the Deity lives in bodily form, and you have been given fullness in Christ, who is the head over every power and authority.

* God has a plan for our lives. But the Enemy also has a plan for our lives—a plan to steal, kill, and destroy.
* Satan is a thief and he wants to steal the treasure that God designed specifically for you.
* If Satan can't keep you from becoming a Christ follower, his next objective is to keep you from discovering and living from your true inheritance.
* When we come to Christ, we are complete. We just need to realize our worth. We have the seal of the King imprinted on our bodies. Our value is beyond comprehension.

As she closes the video message, Chris reminds us that whatever has been stolen from us can be reclaimed, because it's ours. What's been stolen from you? What is it that it is rightfully yours? What do you dream of reclaiming?

SMALL-GROUP DISCUSSION *25-35 minutes

If we read the Bible cover to cover, except for the beginning chapters in Genesis when all is well, we find the condition of humanity in a cycle of perpetual brokenness—either crying out for help or turning their backs on God.

When David stopped to consider all the wonderful works of God in the beginning (Psalm 8), he was amazed that we were created just below God, with great intrinsic value. When Jeremiah looked at the habitual, sinful nature of God's people (Jeremiah 17), he marveled at what the heart of man had become.

PSALM 8:3-5

[3] When I observe Your heavens, the work of Your fingers, the moon and the stars, which You set in place, [4] what is man that You remember him, the son of man that You look after him? [5] You made him little less than God and crowned him with glory and honor.

JEREMIAH 17:9

The heart is more deceitful than anything else, and incurable—who can understand it?

When you read these passages, notice the contrasting thoughts between how God created us in the very beginning and our human nature. We see two distinct pictures of humanity, and both are true. The problem isn't deciding which one is true. The problem is deciding which truth is going to define us.

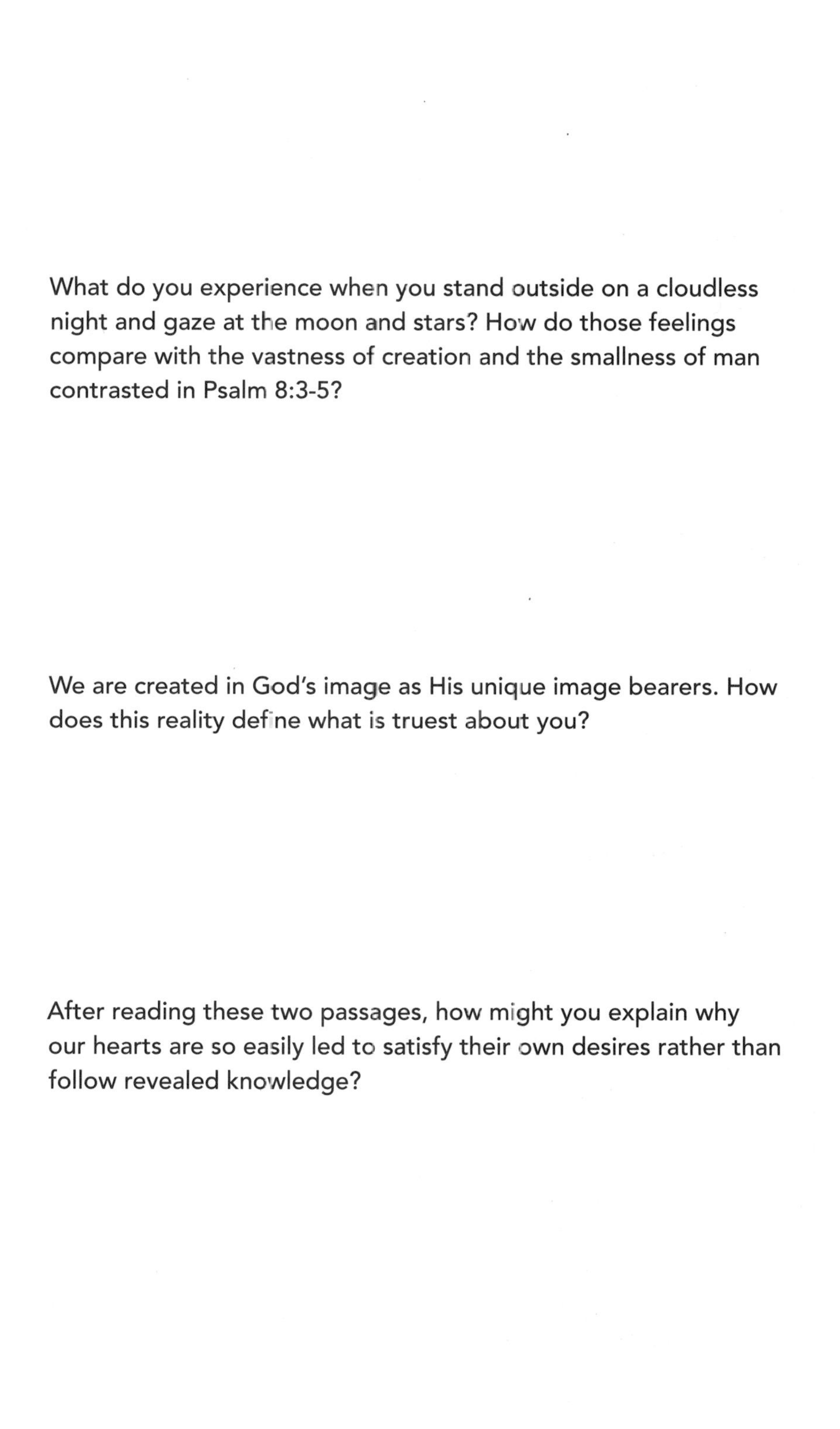

What do you experience when you stand outside on a cloudless night and gaze at the moon and stars? How do those feelings compare with the vastness of creation and the smallness of man contrasted in Psalm 8:3-5?

We are created in God's image as His unique image bearers. How does this reality define what is truest about you?

After reading these two passages, how might you explain why our hearts are so easily led to satisfy their own desires rather than follow revealed knowledge?

Paul wrote about the human condition and God's love. He explains how God relates to us through Jesus Christ in "family" terms. When you read Romans 8:15-17 in light of reclaiming our stolen inheritance, the implications are stunning.

ROMANS 8:15-17

[15] For you did not receive a spirit of slavery to fall back into fear, but you received the Spirit of adoption, ... [16] The Spirit Himself testifies together with our spirit that we are God's children, [17] and if children, also heirs—heirs of God and co-heirs with Christ.

In terms of inheritance, what is the implication of being a co-heir with Christ?

One of the most definitive passages of Scripture about who we are in Christ is found in Ephesians 2. The picture is that of royal sons and daughters rightfully finding our place in the kingdom we have and will inherit. Early in Ephesians 1, Paul proclaims that God raised Christ from the dead and seated "Him at His right hand in the heavens" (Ephesians 1:20). Ephesians 2 reveals even more about our worth to God. Our worth is not based upon our behavior but our true identity—which God has declared over us and restored through Jesus Christ.

EPHESIANS 2:4-7 (NIV)

[4] Because of his great love for us, God, who is rich in mercy, [5] made us alive with Christ even when we were dead in transgressions—it is by grace you have been saved. [6] And God raised us up with Christ and seated us with him in the heavenly realms in Christ Jesus, [7] in order that in the coming ages he might show the incomparable riches of his grace, expressed in his kindness to us in Christ Jesus.

God can declare us worthy and valuable to Him despite what we may believe about ourselves. What tactics does Satan use to convince us otherwise?

What do you need to change about the way you see yourself to align with how God sees you?

Because of Christ's work on the cross, our worth to God and our relationship with Him are back in their proper place. How can we practically live out this inheritance?

WRAP

How do you determine the value of an object? By what someone is willing to pay for it. How much are we worth? Christ thinks we're worth dying for. When we come to Christ, we are complete. God gave us something so inherently valuable that the Enemy will try every trick in his book to steal it from us. But it's ours. And even if it's been stolen, it *can* be reclaimed.

Remember these key thoughts from this week's study:

* God has a plan for our lives. But the Enemy also has a plan for our lives—a plan to steal, kill, and destroy.
* If Satan can't keep you from becoming a Christ follower, his next objective is to keep you from discovering and living from your true inheritance.
* Being a co-heir with Christ means we have full access to God and what He has given His Son.

DEVOTIONAL 1

DON'T BE THAT GUY

What is a man benefited if he gains the whole world, yet loses or forfeits himself? (Luke 9:25)

LORD, You are my portion and my cup of blessing; You hold my future. (Psalm 16:5)

King Edward VIII of England had everything. He was young, famous, rich, and attractive. Edward was born to be king. It was pre-ordained as a matter of birthright. His inheritance was more than any one man could fathom. But his reign was one of the shortest of any British monarch.

Edward met a married American socialite, fell in love, and proposed marriage. In the end, he forfeited his right to be king and gave up all that was rightfully his, convinced that his love was worth losing everything.

The Enemy will try to do the same things to you that King Edward did to himself. Your inheritance is grander than anything you can imagine; yet the Enemy will convince you otherwise if you allow him. Decide now to embrace your godly inheritance, your value, your worth to God.

In what ways have you acted like King Edward?

How has the Enemy convinced you to give up aspects of your spiritual inheritance?

Christ-followers have been born into a better inheritance than any earthly monarchy. We are co-heirs with Jesus Christ, and our inheritance is found in God's kingdom. We are royalty in His eyes. Don't forget your birthright. Don't lose your identity like King Edward did.

DEVOTIONAL 2
PROTECT WHAT'S VALUABLE

[9] For this reason also, since the day we heard this, we haven't stopped praying for you. ... [11] May you be strengthened with all power, according to His glorious might, for all endurance and patience, with joy [12] giving thanks to the Father, who has enabled you to share in the saints' inheritance in the light. [13] He has rescued us from the domain of darkness and transferred us into the kingdom of the Son He loves. [14] We have redemption, the forgiveness of sins, in Him. (Colossians 1:9,11-14)

The Lion, the Witch, and the Wardrobe has inspired and entertained millions since its release. In the novel, we meet four children—unlikely heroes and, though they don't know it, heirs to a vast magical kingdom. They arrive from our own world via a magic wardrobe and into the land of Narnia where it has been prophesied that the sons of Adam and daughters of Eve will occupy the four empty thrones. However, an unnatural winter reigns over the land at the behest of the White Witch, who intends to steal the children's rightful inheritance.

The White Witch tries lies, intimidation, treachery, and even murder. Our Enemy is a more subtle foe. Nonetheless, our adversary wishes to steal our inheritance by any means necessary. His schemes are real. And given the opportunity, he will steal from us what God intends for us to have.

What areas of your life do you feel the Enemy is attempting to sabotage? What actions can you take to reclaim what is yours?

Protect your inheritance by immersing yourself in God's Word. Believe that He has a throne for you. You are a co-heir with Christ. You, in God's eyes, hold more power and more value than Satan. But Satan will attempt to convince you otherwise. Don't believe him.

DEVOTIONAL 3
IF THE SHOE FITS ...

He has made everything beautiful in its time ... yet they cannot fathom what God has done from beginning to end. (Ecclesiastes 3:11, NIV)

[20] Now to Him who is able to do above and beyond all that we ask or think according to the power that works in us— [21] to Him be glory. (Ephesians 3:20-21)

The story of Cinderella is a time-honored tale that fits well with the American cultural mindset—the idea of an underdog who triumphs despite extreme adversity. Rather than enjoying her rightful place in her father's house, she was required to live the life of a servant.

Cinderella is granted a pair of magic slippers and heads to the ball where she dances the night away with a handsome prince—until the clock strikes midnight. In the end Cinderella is revealed as the true princess and ascends into the life for which she was meant.

As sons and daughters of God, we can and will be made beautiful. But unlike Cinderella, we don't need to wait for a pair of magic shoes or our own Prince Charming. We have access to the Prince of Peace Himself, and we can realize our rightful inheritance now.

Have you ever felt unworthy like Cinderella? List obstacles that prevent you from achieving your maximum potential and commit to pray for the strength to overcome them.

Carve out some time this week for you and God. Recognize that He is holding out your very own glass slipper and asking you to join Him. Think about how much you are worth in His eyes. Ask Him to reveal to you just a glimpse of what you could never ask for or imagine.

SESSION 2
STOLEN STRENGTH

The worn-out mom. The battle-weary soldier. The exhausted businessman. The overwhelmed college student. We experience fatigue in many ways and for many reasons. The Enemy has a way of bombarding our lives with troubles, tumult, and distractions. Each of these can zap us physically and weaken us spiritually.

In Matthew 11:28-30, Jesus urges us to get away with Him. If you are feeling the heavy burden of operating outside of God's strength, you are living at an unsustainable pace.

Are you ready to embark on a new journey and set a course correction that puts you on the path to reclaiming your stolen strength? You don't have to live this way any longer.

FLASHBACK

*10 minutes

Use this time to talk with your group about how God has revealed Himself to you since last week's study.

Have you been able to immerse yourself more in God's Word over the past week? If so, how did that time help you move past the obstacles that were keeping you from reclaiming your God/self-worth?

From your devotional time this past week, what was your response to the question—"How has the Enemy convinced you to give up aspects of your spiritual inheritance?"

FRAMING THE STORY

*5-10 minutes

How have you observed business leaders, political leaders, or church leaders exhibit strength in their own right?

What are some different ways we can exhibit strength?

Watch video session 2: "Stolen Strength" (18:00).

REEL TIME

*10 minutes

Fill in the blanks below on important points as you view the message from Kerry and Chris. You'll unpack this information with the group after the video.

Change your focus from what _______________ can't do to what _______________ can do. (Joshua 1:6-9)

"So many times we focus on _______________ that are in front of us — _______________ is impossible with God."

Change your focus from your _________________________ to God's _________________________. (Joshua 1:9b)

Not all things are _________________________, but God can bring good out of the _________________________ _________________________. (Joshua 1:13; Romans 8:28)

Speak in faith regardless of your _________________________. (Joshua 1:10-11)

Act in faith regardless of your _________________________. (Joshua 3:15-16)

In the Christian life, God says, "You get in the _______________ _______________ and _______________.

2 TIMOTHY 1:7, NLT

For God has not given us a spirit of fear and timidity, but of power, love, and self-discipline.

* Satan is waiting to steal our strength and replace it with fear, weakness, and anxiety.
* God wants us to reclaim what's rightfully ours, not be afraid of what might be out there. He wants us to know what our inheritance is and claim it.
* Joshua was feeling weak and afraid, but God moved Joshua from fear to courage.
* When we realize we're stressed and anxious, it's because we've taken the wheel back from God. It's a constant, daily process of moving to the back seat and surrendering to His power and strength.

Which seat are *you* in on your tandem bike? How can you make sure you stay in the back seat?

SMALL-GROUP DISCUSSION *25-35 minutes

Following Christ is a constant struggle, and Paul knew this all too well. Paul planted several churches around the known Mediterranean world. He had suffered hardships of all kinds—physical, emotional, and spiritual. He had completed at least two missionary journeys and was no doubt tired and fatigued from the very work to which Jesus Christ had called him. In one such experience recounted in 2 Corinthians 12, Paul describes what happened when he had finally had enough. He was at the end of his rope, exhausted and weak. Paul needed something to change before he could continue to move forward with God.

2 CORINTHIANS 12:5,7-10

[5] I will boast about this person, but not about myself, except of my weaknesses. ... [7] so that I would not exalt myself, a thorn in the flesh was given to me, a messenger of Satan to torment me so I would not exalt myself. [8] Concerning this, I pleaded with the Lord three times to take it away from me. [9] But He said to me, "My grace is sufficient for you, for power is perfected in weakness." Therefore, I will most gladly boast all the more about my weaknesses, so that Christ's power may reside in me.

[10] So I take pleasure in weaknesses, insults, catastrophes, persecutions, and in pressures, because of Christ. For when I am weak, then I am strong.

Look back at the opening paragraph on page 26. How would you describe Paul's journeys with God so far? What kind of person does he seem to be?

What do you think this "thorn in the flesh" had to do with the Enemy's bid to steal Paul's strength?

Instead of allowing Satan to steal his strength, Paul reacted and took action based on what he knew to be true. What do you think had to transpire within the innermost parts of Paul's heart in order for him to make this decision?

God promised Paul that His grace was sufficient. And Paul was able to rest in that, despite his affliction. Even if we can't see it with our eyes or feel it with our emotions, our love for and faith in God propel us to take Him at His word. When He speaks truth into our lives, we must let that be the driving factor in our minds, hearts, and ultimately our wills. This is when we take action steps of faith and let God do His work to transform us from the inside out, restoring the strength He has given us.

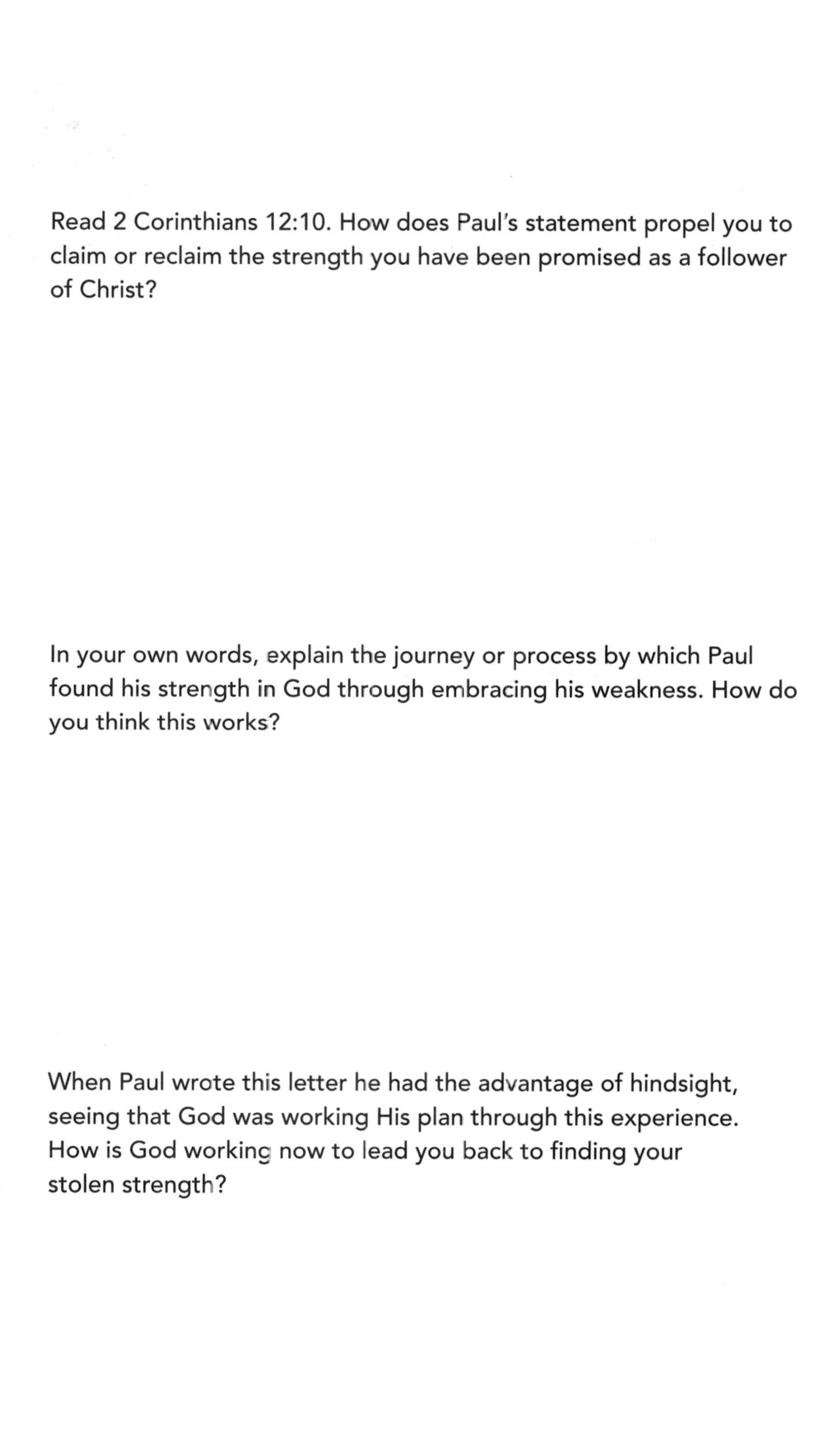

Read 2 Corinthians 12:10. How does Paul's statement propel you to claim or reclaim the strength you have been promised as a follower of Christ?

In your own words, explain the journey or process by which Paul found his strength in God through embracing his weakness. How do you think this works?

When Paul wrote this letter he had the advantage of hindsight, seeing that God was working His plan through this experience. How is God working now to lead you back to finding your stolen strength?

In 2 Corinthians 11, Paul reveals a litany of hardships and dangers he endured throughout his journeys.

2 CORINTHIANS 11:24-29

[24] Five times I received 39 lashes from Jews. [25] Three times I was beaten with rods by the Romans. Once I was stoned by my enemies. Three times I was shipwrecked. I have spent a night and a day in the open sea. [26] On frequent journeys, I faced dangers from rivers, dangers from robbers, dangers from my own people, dangers from the Gentiles, dangers in the city, dangers in the open country, dangers on the sea, and dangers among false brothers; [27] labor and hardship, many sleepless nights, hunger and thirst, often without food, cold, and lacking clothing. [28] Not to mention other things, there is the daily pressure on me: my care for all the churches. [29] Who is weak, and I am not weak? Who is made to stumble, and I do not burn with indignation?

The way we see Paul live out his life in these passages is a reminder that we can't just sit around waiting for God. But we can believe that God "has our back" and gain strength from that truth. So, then, how can we know where our strength ends and His begins?

What past experiences, loss, or wounds has the Enemy used against you to try and steal your strength? Where are you on the path to reclaiming your stolen strength?

WRAP

We can learn so much from the life of Paul. His tenacity for God strengthened him to endure beatings, hardships, and perilous times. But no matter how strong or stubborn the will, there are some things that will leave us empty, weak, and dry if we attempt to handle them in our own strength. Paul never asked God to stop the beatings, shipwrecks, etc. But he did have to surrender what he could not bear on his own.

Remember these key thoughts from this week's study:

* Satan is waiting to steal our strength and replace it with fear, weakness, and anxiety.
* When we realize we're stressed and anxious, it's because we've taken the wheel back from God. It's a constant, daily process of moving to the back seat and surrendering to His power and strength.
* The power source for personal strength is God, but we must be connected to Him in order to receive and utilize that power.
* The Enemy's lies center on this statement: You can control external circumstances and handle it yourself.
* Reclaiming our stolen strength is a process, and it takes time.

DEVOTIONAL 1

FIGHT THE GOOD FIGHT

> [1] Lord, God of my salvation, I cry out before You day and night. [2] May my prayer reach Your presence; listen to my cry. ... [4] I am like a man without strength. (Psalm 88:1-2,4)

> Even there Your hand will lead me; Your right hand will hold on to me. (Psalm 139:10)

For fans of the sport of MMA (Mixed Martial Arts), the name Georges "Rush" St. Pierre is well known. He is widely considered to be one of the best fighters in the game. He is a natural athlete, limited only by the focus in his heart. And his training regimen is world-renowned.

Fast forward to UFC 69 and you see a strong man fall. St. Pierre lost a title fight to a "no name." He let the worries of life distract him just long enough to be defeated. Georges lost that fight because he beat himself.

St. Pierre handled the loss by going back to the fundamentals of his training. He worked through the personal issues in his life and returned to the gym to regain his strength.

What battles have zapped your strength? How has that affected your confidence in God? In yourself?

What spiritual "fundamentals" or disciplines do you need to reincorporate into your daily spiritual regimen?

Wherever you are in your journey with God, He is there. Meditate on Psalm 139 this week. Pray that God will reveal truths you may have forgotten. Ask Him to reveal the pathway back to recovering your strength.

DEVOTIONAL 2
WEAK SPOT

The LORD is my strength and my shield; my heart trusts in Him, and I am helped. Therefore my heart rejoices, and I praise Him with my song. (Psalm 28:7)

Judges 16:17-20 summarizes the story of the biblical strongman who protected the Israelites from the Philistines before the line of the kings. Samson was born under unusual circumstances. His mother was sterile, yet she and her husband were visited by an angel of the Lord who prophesied that not only would they have a son, but he would be a mighty man of great deeds. To ensure this, Samson need only follow the Nazirite vow. In order to be a Nazirite, one had to observe a few strict religious rules. Samson violated these vows repeatedly, yet still retained his power until Delilah cut his hair. Why? Because there were no vows left for Samson to break.

It was only with God's power that Samson was able to do what he did. Without the Spirit of the Lord, we do not have the strength to accomplish anything for Him. Samson took the precious gifts of God for granted—disrespecting and squandering them. And in the end he learned the hard way just how strong he was without God.

Trusting God doesn't mean that we don't do anything. It means trusting that He has given us what we need. To what degree are you attempting to accomplish life in your own power? How is that affecting you?

The Enemy would love nothing more than to steal your strength. God is the ultimate source of that strength; but if Satan can make you forget that simple fact—or disrespect it—he will succeed in weakening your walk. Memorize Psalm 28:7 and use it as a shield against his lies.

DEVOTIONAL 3
NO NEED

[1] The LORD is my shepherd; there is nothing I lack.
[2] He lets me lie down in green pastures;
He leads me beside quiet waters. ...
[4] Even when I go through the darkest valley, ...
You are with me; ...
[6] Only goodness and faithful love will pursue me
all the days of my life. (Psalm 23:1-2,4,6)

In the Lord, we don't lack for anything. But there are a thousand voices calling to us, trying to draw us away from God's guiding hand.

If anyone or anything else is shepherding us, we won't be satisfied. If our careers shepherd us, restlessness and feverish activity will steal our strength. If we look for strength through our achievements, we will constantly be disillusioned. If we rely on other people for our strength, disappointed and unmet expectations will leave us feeling empty.

What outside sources have you been depending on for your strength? How effective have those things been? In what ways do David's words in Psalm 23 provide hope that you can claim your strength from the real Source?

The Enemy may use a lot of different tools to steal our tangible strength, but our true power lies in our relationship with the Lord. Embrace your weakness; for through it God will make known to you strength you never dreamed possible.

Spend time in Psalm 23 this week. It is your shield against all would-be attackers. When all else fails, God will be there to lay you next to green pastures and refresh your soul.

SESSION 3
STOLEN PEACE

In a world where an Enemy is actively seeking to kill and destroy, our peace can be stolen. Restless nights, hours of worry, physical stress—all occupy our spirits and define our reality because there is a relentless evil one who desires to see us fail. And we allow him to take what is rightfully ours.

A few days before Jesus died on the cross and set in motion His journey back to the Father, He told His disciples, "I am leaving you with a gift—peace of mind and heart. And the peace I give is a gift the world cannot give. So don't be troubled or afraid" (John 14:27, NLT).

The disciples did not fully understand what Jesus was saying or how that promise was going to work out. But these things are certain—peace is a valuable gift from God, and we cannot find it seeking after things of this world.

FLASHBACK

*10 minutes

Use this time to talk with your group about how God has revealed Himself to you since last week's study.

What strategic decisions have you made over the past week to operate in God's strength instead of your own?

Which daily devotional experience was most revealing to you? Why?

FRAMING THE STORY

*5-10 minutes

From world peace to inner peace, describe the most peaceful time you have experienced.

What do you think is the biggest obstacle to people experiencing peace in their lives?

Watch video session 3: "Stolen Peace" (16:45).

REEL TIME

*10 minutes

Fill in the blanks below on important points as you view the message from Kerry and Chris.

Counterfeits to peace:

We look for peace in our ___________________________.

We look for peace in being ___________________________.

If you're outside of God's will, you'll have no

______________________.

In the middle of ____________________ ____________________

is the safest place we could be.

How do we reclaim our peace?

Trust in the security of God's ___________________________

Trust in the security of God's ___________________________

Trust in the security of God's ___________________________

JOHN 14:27

"Peace I leave with you. My peace I give to you. I do not give to you as the world gives. Your heart must not be troubled or fearful."

PSALM 20:7

Some take pride in chariots, and others in horses,
but we take pride in the name of Yahweh our God.

PHILIPPIANS 4:7

And the peace of God, which surpasses every thought, will guard your hearts and your minds in Christ Jesus.

* Peace is one of the greatest gifts ever given to us by God.
* God doesn't call us to live a comfortable life, He calls us to live a passionate life.
* God doesn't want us filled with despair or worry. He doesn't want us to be paralyzed by the circumstances of our lives. Instead, He provides a way for us to move forward through the turbulent waters.

Where is your heart right now? Are you at peace? Filled with anxiety? Flooded with fears?

What counterfeits are you pursuing in place of true peace?

SMALL-GROUP DISCUSSION *25-35 minutes

If we eliminate our risk, we can erase our problems, right? To believe this, we would have to truly believe that our peace could be attained by our own strength—that we actually have the power to control everything around us. But consider this: the very nature of the existence of the Enemy and his desire to destroy us invites the risk of hardship and turmoil. Interestingly enough, there is no single book, chapter, or verse in Scripture that reveals a guaranteed plan to escape the hardships of life. It doesn't exist. There are, however, passages of Scripture that teach us what it means to find the hidden treasures of God no matter the circumstances in our lives.

1 PETER 1:3-9

[3] Praise the God and Father of our Lord Jesus Christ. According to His great mercy, He has given us a new birth into a living hope through the resurrection of Jesus Christ from the dead [4] and into an inheritance that is imperishable, uncorrupted, and unfading, kept in heaven for you. [5] You are being protected by God's power through faith for a salvation that is ready to be revealed in the last time. [6] You rejoice in this, though now for a short time you have had to struggle in various trials [7] so that the genuineness of your faith—more valuable than gold, which perishes though refined by fire—may result in praise, glory, and honor at the revelation of Jesus Christ. [8] You love Him, though you have not seen Him. And though not seeing Him now, you believe in Him and rejoice with inexpressible and glorious joy, [9] because you are receiving the goal of your faith, the salvation of your souls.

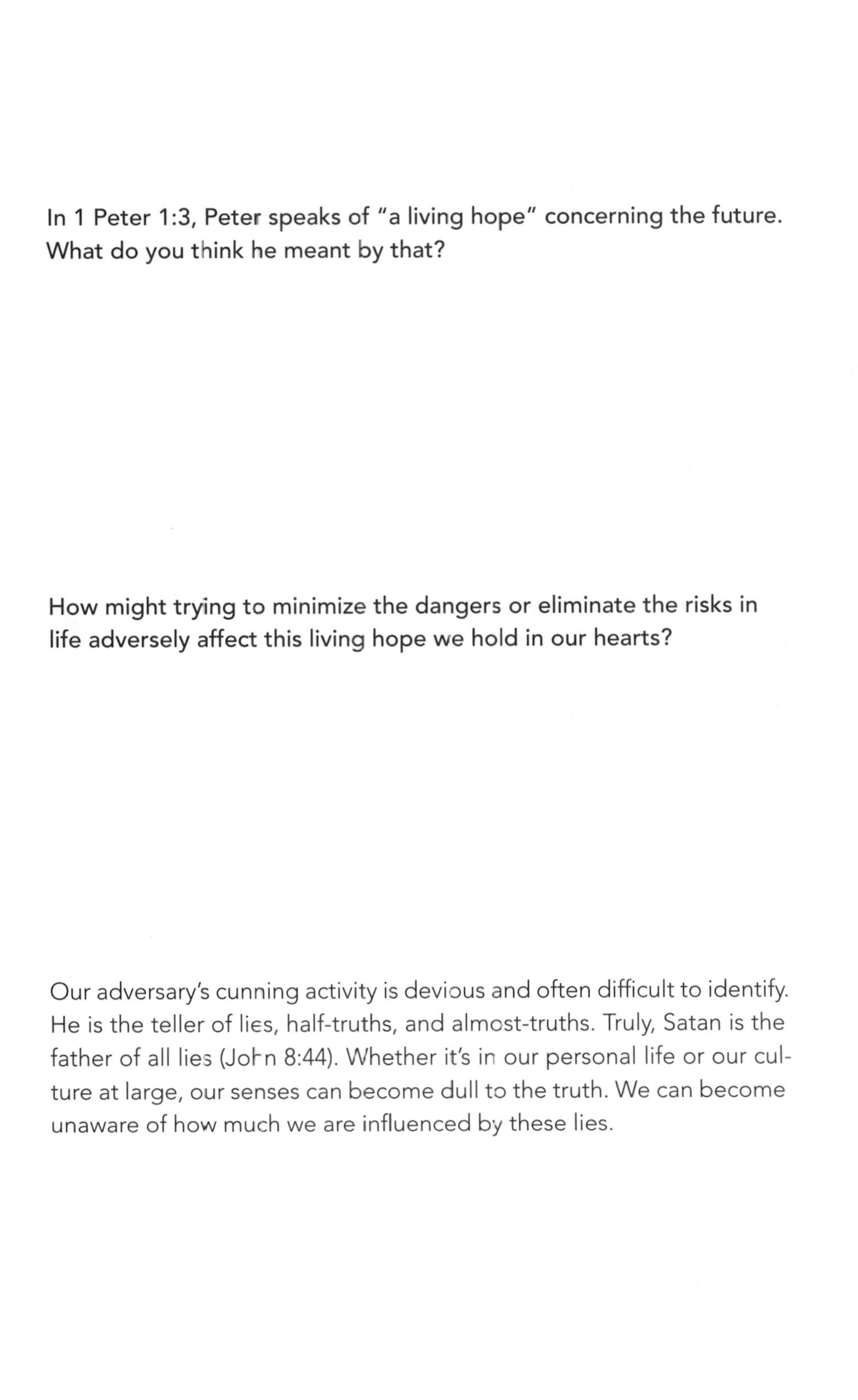

In 1 Peter 1:3, Peter speaks of "a living hope" concerning the future. What do you think he meant by that?

How might trying to minimize the dangers or eliminate the risks in life adversely affect this living hope we hold in our hearts?

Our adversary's cunning activity is devious and often difficult to identify. He is the teller of lies, half-truths, and almost-truths. Truly, Satan is the father of all lies (John 8:44). Whether it's in our personal life or our culture at large, our senses can become dull to the truth. We can become unaware of how much we are influenced by these lies.

In what ways do we act out our belief in the lie that if we avoid hardship at any cost we will find peace?

First Peter 1:3-9 describes our inheritance, strength, and joy mostly from the perspective of our future—when these treasures will be restored in their fullest capacity. But verse 5 states that we "are being protected" right now. What do you think God wants you to experience under His protection?

So far in our study together we have discussed some common themes—the treasure we have lost, the schemes of the Enemy, the journey back to God, and understanding who God has created us to be. Grasping the truth of who we really are significantly relates to all the other themes. This understanding is what gives us the ability to interpret our circumstances in light of the Divine meaning behind them.

Peter speaks of a reward in 1 Peter 1:9. The "salvation of your souls"—the innermost parts of who we are, our identity and existence—will not be destroyed. How does resting on this promise give you the courage to embrace your circumstances, to claim your peace?

Verse 7 talks about "the genuineness of your faith" in facing trials. What else do our reactions to trials reveal about what we really believe? How can these revelations help us navigate our way back to reclaiming our stolen peace?

Throughout his life, Peter came to understand the cost of persecution first hand. He was beaten and jailed several times while living for God. Church tradition holds that he, too, was crucified like his Lord. Except Peter, per his request, was hung upside-down because he felt unworthy to suffer in the same manner as Jesus. Knowing this about Peter makes these words that much more inspiring:

1 PETER 4:12-14

[12] Dear friends, don't be surprised when the fiery ordeal comes among you to test you as if something unusual were happening to you. [13] Instead, rejoice as you share in the sufferings of the Messiah, so that you may also rejoice with great joy at the revelation of His glory. [14] If you are ridiculed for the name of Christ, you are blessed, because the Spirit of glory and of God rests on you.

In verse 13 Peter says to "rejoice as you share in the sufferings." How might this differ from denying our pain and suffering? Describe it.

What kind of peace do you imagine you will experience when the Spirit of God "rests" upon you? Describe.

WRAP

According to Peter, Christ-followers need not be surprised when they experience trials and suffering. Twice Peter used the image of fire to communicate the risk and reward of following Christ (1 Peter 1:7; 4:12). Fiery ordeals will test us as flames test and purify gold. Even in the middle of the fire, our faith is not consumed. Rather, it is strengthened and the peace of God is ours to experience.

Remember these key thoughts from this week's study:

* Peace is one of the greatest gifts ever given to us by God.
* God doesn't want us filled with despair or worry. Instead, He provides a way for us to move forward through the turbulent waters.
* Trying to eliminate the risk of hardship does not guarantee peace.
* Constantly insulating ourselves from "the more difficult" may, in the long run, actually weaken our faith and hope in God.
* The pathway to peace is always ready to be walked despite the turbulent circumstances around us.

DEVOTIONAL 1

A LITTLE PEACE OF HEAVEN

Therefore, we may boldly say: The Lord is my helper; I will not be afraid. What can man do to me? (Hebrews 13:6)

[18] If I say, "My foot is slipping," Your faithful love will support me, LORD. [19] When I am filled with cares, Your comfort brings me joy. (Psalm 94:18-19)

The economy continues to tank. The housing market is in shambles. War rages in the Middle East. Hurricanes, tsunamis, wildfires, tornadoes. Our culture seems embroiled in the decadence, self indulgence, and godlessness that has preceded the fall of every major civilization in human history. And if we just focused on these things every day, peace would be fleeting ... to say the least.

When fear whispers in our hearts—stealing our resolve and our peace—our instinct is to hunker down and wait until it blows over. Remember when Jesus and His disciples were on the Sea of Galilee and the storm arose? Jesus walked on the water, and the initial reaction of the disciples was fear. He replied to them, "'Why are you fearful, you of little faith?' Then He got up and rebuked the winds and the sea. And there was a great calm" (Matthew 8:26).

"Do not fear, for I am with you" (Isaiah 41:10). The Lord is on your side.

What excuses have you used for surrendering your peace to the adversary? What actions do you feel God is calling you to take to reclaim the peace that is rightfully yours?

Determine today that no matter what issues arise, you will meet them bravely with God's help.

DEVOTIONAL 2
ARE YOU KARATE KIDDIN' ME?

Turn away from evil and do what is good; seek peace and pursue it. (Psalm 34:14)

You will keep the mind that is dependent on You in perfect peace, for it is trusting in You. (Isaiah 26:3)

The *Karate Kid* opens on Daniel LaRusso and his mother moving from New Jersey to California. He is plainly upset, continuing a running diatribe about everything from the unasked-for move to their station wagon to their new apartment complex. With every difficulty, Daniel's annoyance grows and his peace is threatened. Daniel has no inner calm, and it shows in his outward demeanor.

We often find ourselves in the midst of a similar situation. Chaos rules around us. We are consistently thwarted in our attempts to control our environments. We believe if we can control our circumstances, we will no longer be troubled by the world.

In the movie, Daniel was able to achieve inner peace through his training with Mr. Miyagi. For us, we need to pursue a life in which our peace is bound with the Savior, in the sure knowledge that all rests in His hands and no matter what life throws our way, He will be there to see us through.

How do you react to the stresses of life? In what ways do your reactions manifest themselves on the outside?

Spend some time this week identifying what you need to alter in your life to keep you focused on the inner peace that only God can give. When the busyness of live consumes you, develop a consistent strategy to help you focus on God and allow you to reclaim your stolen peace.

DEVOTIONAL 3
WE ARE THE WORLD

> [44] But I tell you, love your enemies and pray for those who persecute you, [45] so that you may be sons of your Father in heaven. For He causes His sun to rise on the evil and the good, and sends rain on the righteous and the unrighteous. (Matthew 5:44-45)

In a world full of war, hate, misery, and racial tension, we can sometimes forget that God considers world peace of the utmost importance. C. S. Lewis said, "God cannot give us a happiness and peace apart from Himself, because it is not there. There is no such thing."[1] A right relationship with our God is the beginning of the journey if we want to attain peace in our world. Before any man can ask peace of another, he must first have peace within himself. His soul must not be at odds with God.

We pursue peace in our lives not just for its own sake, but also as a means to further God's kingdom here on earth. This is why the Enemy is relentless and takes so much pleasure in stealing our peace—it's valuable not just to you, but to the ones with whom you share it.

What does the "world at peace" look like to you? Since world peace starts in your circle, with whom do you need to make peace?

It's not enough to seek and find it. When you attain the peace of God in your life, what are you going to do with it?

Find someone with whom you harbor a grudge and forgive him or her. Do it honestly. Then stand back and watch God's hand at work.

1. C. S. Lewis, *Mere Christianity* (New York: HarperCollins Publishers, 2001), 50.

SESSION 4
STOLEN DREAMS

Astronauts have walked on the moon. Athletes have shattered Olympic world records. Inventors have created new products. Entrepreneurs have started new businesses. Explorers have discovered new worlds, new planets. Free nations have been founded. Storytellers have made movies. Scientists have discovered new breakthroughs. Doctors have performed groundbreaking surgeries.

Don't underestimate the power of a dream. Don't underestimate the power of pursuing that dream.

Maybe your dreams have been abandoned, forgotten, stolen. It doesn't matter how big your dream feels. If it's God's dream for you, then it's huge! Heaven only knows where you will go and what you will experience when you begin to pursue your stolen dreams once again.

FLASHBACK

*10 minutes

Use this time to talk with your group about how God has revealed Himself to you since last week's study.

Because of the worry and stress of everyday life, true peace can be elusive. Take a moment to share and celebrate any victories you have experienced related to reclaiming your stolen peace.

From your devotional time this past week, what was your response to the question—"How do you react to the stresses of life? In what ways do your reactions manifest themselves on the outside?"

FRAMING THE STORY

*5-10 minutes

How would you define "living the dream"?

What person (past or present, famous or not) do you admire for pursuing his or her dreams? What characteristics or qualities does this person embody?

Watch video session 4: "Stolen Dreams" (18:00).

REEL TIME

*10 minutes

Fill in the blanks below on important points as you view the message from Kerry and Chris.

The difference between dream and fantasy:

Dream includes all the ____________, ____________, and ____________.

Fantasy is all ____________, no ____________, no work, no substance.

When we guard our hearts, it's also important that we don't ____________ our hearts down and ________________ our dreams.

One of the ways the Enemy paralyzes us is with ____________________.

Three fears that paralyze us from pursuing our dreams:

Fear of the ________________________________

Fear of ____________________________________

Fear of ____________________________________

How do we know if a dream is from God?

It's bigger than our ______________________.

It's ______________________________.

It will match our ______________________.

It will always align with God's ________________ ________________.

PROVERBS 14:18, THE MESSAGE

Foolish dreamers live in a world of illusion;
wise realists plant their feet on the ground.

PROVERBS 4:23

Guard your heart above all else,
for it is the source of life.

EPHESIANS 3:20

Now to Him who is able to do above and beyond all that we ask or think according to the power that works in us.

* One of the reasons we don't pursue our dreams is because of a wound from the past.
* The enemy will steal our dreams from us and replace them with a counterfeit.
* Fantasy = the enemy's counterfeit to our true, God-given dream.
* We guard our hearts because our dreams are planted there by God.
* When we guard our hearts, we can more easily recognize when the Enemy comes to steal our dreams.

What counterfeits have replaced your true, God-given dreams? What questions do you have about pursuing your dreams? What dream is on your heart that you've never taken a step to claim or reclaim?

SMALL-GROUP DISCUSSION *25-35 minutes

In 2 Kings 4, we find a Shunammite woman who has given up on her dreams. She is described as being wealthy, but she has no children and her husband is old. Undoubtedly she knows about the miraculous conception of Abraham and Sarah's son, Isaac. But when given the opportunity to honestly share what it is she really wants, she refuses to even bring up the subject. Her conversation with the prophet Elisha reveals the true condition of her heart.

2 KINGS 4:11-16, NIV

[11] One day when Elisha came, he went up to his room and lay down there. [12] He said to his servant Gehazi, "Call the Shunammite." So he called her, and she stood before him. [13] Elisha said to him, "Tell her, 'You have gone to all this trouble for us. Now what can be done for you? Can we speak on your behalf to the king or the commander of the army?'" She replied, "I have a home among my own people." [14] "What can be done for her?" Elisha asked. Gehazi said, "Well, she has no son and her husband is old." [15] Then Elisha said, "Call her." So he called her, and she stood in the doorway. [16] "About this time next year," Elisha said, "you will hold a son in your arms." "No, my lord," she objected. "Don't mislead your servant, O man of God!"

When the Shunammite woman was asked if she wanted anything, she avoided the question altogether. Why do you think she didn't answer truthfully?

Financially, the woman was living better than those around her, but she and her husband had been unable to conceive. In what ways do we mask the wounds of stolen dreams in our everyday lives with counterfeits?

Controllable "safe" dreams

God did give the woman a son. But later in the passage, the story reveals that the boy died while out in the fields. He was probably 8 or 9 years old at the time. The woman was devastated, and her grief compelled her to seek out Elisha.

2 KINGS 4:27-28, NIV

[27] When she reached the man of God at the mountain, she took hold of his feet. Gehazi came over to push her away, but the man of God said, "Leave her alone! She is in bitter distress, but the LORD has hidden it from me and has not told me why." [28] "Did I ask you for a son, my lord?" she said. "Didn't I tell you, 'Don't raise my hopes'?"

The first words from the woman to Elisha were, "Did I ask you for a son? ... Didn't I tell you, 'Don't raise my hopes'?" What does this reveal to you about the fragile state of the heart even when our dreams come true?

How do you think the enemy takes advantage of the Shunammite woman's frustration to rob her of hope and desire?

Later in the 2 Kings 4 passage, the Shunammite woman's son was brought back to life. She experienced the truth that God can breathe new life into that which dies. How can this account stir an old longing or dream in you?

Unlike the hesitant Shunammite woman, Peter was willing to literally jump out of the boat in pursuit of his dreams. Before encountering Jesus, Peter's dreams probably centered on his personal life—his family and business. Maybe he dreamt of being the best husband, dad, and commercial fisherman he could be. Regardless of his personal ambitions, it is doubtful that Peter actually fulfilled a lifelong dream when he jumped out of the boat and walked on water that night. But Peter's personal journey toward following Christ included the opportunity to do just that. Even though Peter was impulsive at times, he was not afraid to jump out of the boat when Jesus spoke to his heart.

MATTHEW 14:27-30

[27] Immediately Jesus spoke to them. "Have courage! It is I. Don't be afraid."

[28] "Lord, if it's You," Peter answered Him, "command me to come to You on the water." [29] "Come!" He said. And climbing out of the boat, Peter started walking on the water and came toward Jesus. [30] But when he saw the strength of the wind, he was afraid. And beginning to sink he cried out, "Lord, save me!"

Consider how the disciples reacted to seeing Peter walk on water. What similar feelings do you experience when you see someone taking a step toward pursuing his or her passion?

Sometimes it's not really about the dream itself. It's about what God reveals to us along the way. How do you think reframing the pursuit of your dreams in this way would shape your journey?

What do you think would happen if you were to determine to take back the ground Satan has stolen and allow God's dreams for your life to stir your heart with renewed excitement? Where might those dreams take you?

WRAP

Have your dreams been abandoned, forgotten, stolen, replaced with a counterfeit? Give yourself permission to dream again. Don't underestimate the power of pursuing what God has placed in your heart. God wants us to guard our hearts, but He also wants us to pursue our dreams. He has plans for our lives that are greater than anything we could ask or imagine. And we can join Him there as we live out our God-given dreams.

Remember these key thoughts from this week's study:

* The enemy will steal our dreams from us and replace them with a counterfeit.
* We guard our hearts because our dreams are planted there by God.
* Following your God-given dreams will help you follow God.
* There are real consequences for not following or reclaiming your God-given dreams.
* The journey is just as important as the dream itself.

DEVOTIONAL 1
YOU'RE SO VAIN . . . YOU PROBABLY THINK MY DREAM IS ABOUT YOU

[14] I pursue as my goal the prize promised by God's heavenly call in Christ Jesus. [15] Therefore, all who are mature should think this way. And if you think differently about anything, God will reveal this also to you. [16] In any case, we should live up to whatever truth we have attained. (Philippians 3:14-16)

"Are you really going to reign over us?" his brothers asked him. "Are you really going to rule us?" So they hated him even more because of his dream and what he had said. (Genesis 37:8)

While Joseph's dream came in the form of a literal dream, it was no different than the dreams and ambitions we hold for ourselves if they are godly in origin. Cherish the hardships, the contentious friends, and even the setbacks. The reward will be all the more worth having, and His glory will be that much more as well.

Each one of us has dreams within our hearts, and if we do not guard and cultivate them, they will die. We can only change right now—not yesterday, not tomorrow. What are you doing today to identify your dreams and what they represent?

When the Enemy tries to steal your dreams through the envy of others, remember Paul's words in Philippians 3:14-16 and consider how that moment at the end of the race will feel if you reclaim your stolen dreams in spite of what others may think or say.

DEVOTIONAL 2
NOT ALWAYS AS IT APPEARS

I have asked one thing from the LORD; it is what I desire: to dwell in the house of the LORD all the days of my life, gazing on the beauty of the LORD and seeking Him in His temple. (Psalm 27:4)

This was King David's dream. Who wouldn't want to live in God's house, and be in His presence? Unfortunately, there was a problem. David wished to seek the Lord in the temple, only there wasn't a temple yet.

[2] The king said to Nathan the prophet, "Look, I am living in a cedar house while the ark of God sits inside tent curtains." [3] So Nathan told the king, "Go and do all that is on your heart, for the LORD is with you." (2 Samuel 7:2-3)

[8] But the word of the LORD came to me: "You have shed much blood and waged great wars. You are not to build a house for My name … [9] But a son will be born to you; … [10] He is the one who will build a house for My name." (1 Chronicles 22:8-10)

Unfortunately for David, God had different plans in mind. David didn't get upset. Instead, he saw to the heart of his dream and placed the details of its fulfillment in the Lord's hands. The heart of the dream—the building of the temple—was the same. Only the details had changed.

What do you believe God thinks about your dream? Explain.

God desires your happiness and has plans for your dreams to come true. Are you willing to change the details of your dream if the heart of it remains the same? Spend some time this week reexamining your own dreams.

DEVOTIONAL 3

DREAM . . . DETERMINATION . . . ACTION!

In the same way faith, if it doesn't have works, is dead by itself. (James 2:17)

"For I know the plans I have for you," declares the LORD, "plans to prosper you and not to harm you, plans to give you hope and a future." (Jeremiah 29:11, NIV)

Some movies seem to stand the test of time better than others. The message of the film, its story, and the characters that inspired us resonate as much today as they did the first time we saw them on the silver screen.

Rocky holds such a spot in many of our hearts. This modern-day David and Goliath story struck a chord within us. The first movie's surprise ending—leaving Rocky in immediate defeat yet victorious for having gone the distance—inspired us to fight for our dreams no matter the odds.

Frederick Douglass, an escaped slave who became a famous orator and statesman in the fight against slavery, once said, "I prayed for 20 years but received no answer until I prayed with my legs." In the end it was Douglass's determination and faith in action that made his dream reality.

If you were watching a movie about yourself, what would *you* want *you* to do? Why?

Begin to imagine yourself working toward your dream. Do something today to pray "with your legs." God has given the dream and laid the plans. All that's needed is your effort.

SESSION 5
STOLEN JOY

Killjoy. Someone who deliberately spoils the fun and enjoyment of others through resentful behavior. A party pooper. Someone you don't want to be around.

Our Enemy has made a good living off of being a killjoy. He knows he has already been defeated, but his miserable existence continues to spread chaos. Remember the old saying, "Misery loves company"? The only way the Enemy can enjoy your company is if he steals your joy first.

The word *joy* is mentioned hundreds of times in the Bible. We were meant to live this life with joy—real joy. Consider that Satan may have stolen some of your joy without you even realizing it. Decide that you will pursue God's joy once again, and let today be the beginning of a new journey.

FLASHBACK

*10 minutes

Use this time to talk with your group about how God has revealed Himself to you since last week's study.

Since we met last week, what lost or stolen dreams have been rekindled in your heart?

What plans have you made to pursue them once again?

FRAMING THE STORY

*5-10 minutes

What factors do you think indicate to you that a person is experiencing true joy in life?

What other attitudes or actions do you think are most commonly associated with joy?

Watch video session 5: "Stolen Joy" (14:30).

REEL TIME

*10 minutes

Fill in the blanks below on important points as you view the message from Kerry and Chris. You'll unpack this information with the group after the video.

Counterfeit to joy = ______________________

True joy is deeper than our ______________________.

Joy isn't ______________________ by our circumstances.

Joy is a ______________________ from God, but we have to ______________________ it.

Joy goes deeper than our ______________________.

GALATIANS 5:22-23

The fruit of the Spirit is love, joy, peace, patience, kindness, goodness, faith, gentleness, self-control. Against such things there is no law.

JAMES 1:2-4

Consider it a great joy, my brothers, whenever you experience various trials, knowing that the testing of your faith produces endurance. But endurance must do its complete work, so that you may be mature and complete, lacking nothing.

* Joy is given by God and is much deeper than happiness.
* Every time circumstances come up in our lives, we have a choice—we can choose joy or we can choose to look at the circumstances.
* Happiness is about what's going on on the outside of our lives and joy is what God gives us on the inside.

In the video message, Kerry talked about the "someday syndrome." How has this phenomenon robbed you of your joy?

Are you fighting God, searching for a sense of happiness that seems elusive, or are you resting in Him, trusting God for true joy? Explain.

SMALL-GROUP DISCUSSION *25-35 minutes

It's easy to give God credit when all is well, when life is good, when things are going our way. But it seems to be a little more difficult to give Him credit if we disagree with the circumstances of our lives. And to a certain degree, it goes against human nature to accept the notion that God would actually allow hardships to enter our lives just so He could work His purposes. But when we read John 9, an account where Jesus gives vision to a man who was blind from birth, Jesus makes it clear that the man's blindness had a specific purpose—that God be known.

JOHN 9:1-3

[1] As He was passing by, He saw a man blind from birth. [2] His disciples questioned Him: "Rabbi, who sinned, this man or his parents, that he was born blind?" [3] "Neither this man nor his parents sinned," Jesus answered. "This came about so that God's works might be displayed in him.

Based on the question in verse 2, how would you describe the misconceptions of the disciples?

Jesus' response was intended to shift the disciples' focus from the man's suffering to God's purposes. Why do you think that was important?

We all have preconceived ideas about who God is. From the beginning, each one of us has a different story to tell. These stories are shaped by our family background, social upbringing, past religious experiences, the Enemy's activity, and what we have chosen to believe is true based on all these things.

What do you think is the main difference between blaming God and crediting God? What affect do you think your understanding of each has on your ability to maintain joy?

In what way does accepting that God allows trials and hardships give you permission and freedom to reclaim your stolen joy in life?

In Romans 5, the apostle Paul defends the actions and sovereignty of God and in doing so provides a blueprint of sorts for reclaiming our stolen joy. This passage seems to cut through the temporal happenings of this life and get right to the true reality of how God allows the more difficult things in our lives to achieve His purposes. If our circumstances aren't going to change, then how we see God in our circumstances needs to surface in our minds and hearts. This is where our joy is reclaimed.

ROMANS 5:2-5

[2] We rejoice in the hope of the glory of God. [3] And not only that, but we also rejoice in our afflictions, because we know that affliction produces endurance, [4] endurance produces proven character, and proven character produces hope.
[5] This hope will not disappoint us, because God's love has been poured out in our hearts through the Holy Spirit who was given to us.

Paul uses the term "rejoice" which literally means, "find joy again." What does this reveal to you about the journey ahead?

How do you think developing endurance, character, and hope (v. 4) can lead you on the path to reclaiming your stolen joy?

In the Romans 5 passage, Paul makes it clear that God paves the way for peace, and He is the source of our joy. But we are responsible for aggressively cooperating with God by faith to seek out and find that joy. Reclaiming our stolen joy grants us access to a front-row seat to see God's plans and purposes unfold before our very eyes.

How can you see God's purposes working in your life through hardships and trials? Why do you think God would choose to work this way?

Where are you on this journey? If the Enemy has stolen your joy, where does the shift from "blame God" to "credit God" begin for you?

God meant for us to live this life with joy—real joy. Sometimes Satan steals our joy without us even realizing it. Sometimes we pursue happiness instead and then realize how fleeting that is. Our circumstances may or may not change. But our Source of true joy *never* changes. And He's waiting for us to step up and reclaim our stolen joy.

Remember these key thoughts from this week's study:

* Joy is given by God and is much deeper than happiness.
* Every time circumstances come up in our lives, we have a choice—we can choose joy or we can choose to look at the circumstances.
* Happiness is about what's going on on the outside of our lives and joy is what God gives us on the inside.
* God is at work in our lives in the good times and the bad.

DEVOTIONAL 1

DON'T BELIEVE IT

"The marvelous richness of human experience would lose something of rewarding joy if there were no limitations to overcome. The hilltop hour would not be half so wonderful if there were no dark valleys to traverse." —Helen Keller

So you also have sorrow now. But I will see you again. Your hearts will rejoice, and no one will rob you of your joy. (John 16:22)

What Dreams May Come centers on married couple Chris and Annie Nielsen and the losses they encounter in life. First, they lose their children to a car accident that sends Annie into a volatile depression. And the final blow comes when Chris is killed in a car accident. Annie succumbs to her depression and commits suicide. She lost her joy because she was paralyzed by the grief, and she allowed the circumstances to define her reality in the future.

Events like this happen every day. When our joy is stolen, there is an empty place inside that needs filling. The Adversary is quick to embed deceitful lies about the reality of our situation. And if we believe those lies, we will act on them and become resentful toward God, isolated from those who love us or soothing the emotional pain with something earthly, creating only a momentary solution.

In the movie, Annie's joy was stolen from her. Have you ever felt this way? How did you deal with it?

Spend some time in prayer this week. Ask God to identify any lies the Enemy has embedded in your heart. Memorize John 16:22. Ask God to help you overcome any obstacles in your way as you seek to reclaim your stolen joy.

DEVOTIONAL 2
SOMETHING'S GOTTA GIVE

> [11] I've learned by now to be quite content whatever my circumstances. [12] I'm just as happy with little as with much, with much as with little.... [13] I can make it through anything in the One who makes me who I am. (Philippians 4:11-13, The Message)

The iconic Grinch stands at the heart of every Christmas season, subtly rebuking us of the horrors of commercialism related to our beloved holiday. Every year we watch, we laugh, and we impart this lesson to our children. But who really wishes to steal our joy? Who is happiest when we are most miserable? Satan. And to be honest, he's gotten very good at it. While Dr. Seuss's Grinch steals gifts, trees, and a roast beast feast, our Enemy steals our creature comforts in an attempt to bring us low. Perhaps it's the loss of a comfortable job. Maybe the car breaks down, the furnace leaks, or the bathroom floods. Satan seems to delight in bogging us down in the mundane, all the while subtly suggesting that our joy, or lack thereof, springs from material things.

How have material possessions gotten in the way of you experiencing true joy?

The next time you find yourself upset because of the lack of material possessions, picture Satan as the Grinch. If we learn the lesson of contentment like Paul (Philippians 4:11-13), then the Enemy's schemes will seem silly and ineffectual.

Consider choosing a valuable possession that you think you can't do without and give it to someone less fortunate. Take joy in the pleasure of generous giving. Pray this week, asking God to help you get on the offensive and initiate this battle instead of reacting to it.

DEVOTIONAL 3
ALTERED EGO

Do not be conformed to this age, but be transformed by the renewing of your mind, so that you may discern what is the good, pleasing, and perfect will of God. (Romans 12:2)

"The only One around here not doing His job is You!"
— A frustrated Bruce Nolan speaking to God in *Bruce Almighty* (Universal Pictures, 2003)

In the movie *Bruce Almighty,* Jim Carrey plays a popular television reporter who has a great career and a devoted, loving girlfriend. Despite this, he is not happy with his life or with God.

After Bruce angrily ridicules and rages against Him, God gives Bruce a chance to live the life of the Almighty and make things right. God gives Bruce divine powers to use however he sees fit. Interestingly though, God informs Bruce of two things he cannot do with his powers—he can't tell people that he's God and he can't mess with free will.

When John the Baptist was preaching his message, it was plain and simple. "Change your life. God's kingdom is here" (Matthew 3:2, The Message). We can't "mess with free will" and change others so we can find true joy. The only people we can change are ourselves.

Are you wasting time trying to change other people? In what ways might you be wrapping too much of your joy around somebody else?

When you can't change others, you are left only to change yourself. Take some time to think about what really needs to change in your life for you to reclaim your true joy.

SESSION 6
STOLEN PASSION

We wouldn't cheer for our favorite team if they played with apathy. We wouldn't pay to see a passionless performance of Shakespeare. We wouldn't enjoy a lackluster lecture from those trained in public speaking. We wouldn't walk down the aisle to hear a half-hearted "I do."

We expect professional athletes to play like they are the best. We expect sold-out performances, dynamic speeches, heart-felt wedding vows. We expect more.

God expects more, too. He is the One who gave us the gift of passion. If our life is a stage and God is our audience, what kind of performance can we give Him? If the Enemy has stolen our passion for life, we won't be the only one who notices.

FLASHBACK

*10 minutes

Use this time to talk with your group about how God has revealed Himself to you since last week's study.

In your pursuit of true joy, what false realities of happiness have you been able to identify and destroy?

What specific truths from last week's devotional readings have enabled you to trust God more with your circumstances so you can reclaim your stolen joy?

FRAMING THE STORY

*5-10 minutes

How can you tell when a person is passionate about something?

Where do you think passion comes from?

Watch video session 6: "Stolen Passion" (18:00).

REEL TIME

*10 minutes

Fill in the blanks below on important points as you view the message from Kerry and Chris. You'll unpack this information with the group after the video.

Passion is the difference between ______________________

and ______________________.

Passion is the difference between ______________________

and ______________________.

When Satan steals our passion, he also steals our

______________________.

______________________ people change the world.

How we can reclaim our stolen passion:

Spend time ______________________ with God. (1 Kings 17:3)

Decide not to ____________________ the fence. (1 Kings 18:21)

Repair the ______________________ in your life (1 Kings 18:30)

______________________ always produces passion.

Live so that only _____________ gets the glory. (1 Kings 18:37)

ECCLESIASTES 3:11

He has ... put eternity in their hearts.

* Jesus will redeem what's been stolen from us so we can reclaim our treasures.
* God wants us to have the fire of passion in our lives.
* Something within us desires to live for something greater than ourselves.
* God wants us to have deep convictions because convictions are the foundation for the flame of passion.

Kerry and Chris shared four actions we can take to reclaim our passion. Which resonated with you most? Explain your response to the group.

How do you describe someone who is living with passion?

What motivates you? Do you want God's glory more than anything else? Would you say your motivation is more internal or eternal?

SMALL-GROUP DISCUSSION *25-35 minutes

Passion is found throughout Scripture. We see it lived out in those who wanted to truly experience life. One such example is found in a story told by Jesus. Couched within a series of parables concerning what has been lost, we find a story in the Gospels about a father and his two sons. The youngest son left the father to experience life. It was this son's passion for life, although misguided and without direction, that motivated him from the very beginning.

LUKE 15:11-14

[11] "A man had two sons. [12] The younger of them said to his father, 'Father, give me the share of the estate I have coming to me.' So he distributed the assets to them. [13] Not many days later, the younger son gathered together all he had and traveled to a distant country, where he squandered his estate in foolish living. [14] After he had spent everything, a severe famine struck that country, and he had nothing.

What kind of passionate impulses, crazy thoughts, or deep desires do you think existed in the younger son when he made his request for his share of his father's estate?

What mistakes did the prodigal son make? Did he get anything right? Explain.

The younger son went off to chase his desires, but the older son never left the father. After a period of time and the realization that his father had better things in store for him than he could achieve on his own, the prodigal son returned home. The father ran to him, embraced him, and threw a massive party.

LUKE 15:25-32

[25] Now his older son was in the field; as he came near the house, he heard music and dancing. [26] So he summoned one of the servants and asked what these things meant. [27] "Your brother is here," he told him, "and your father has slaughtered the fattened calf because he has him back safe and sound."

[28] Then he became angry and didn't want to go in. So his father came out and pleaded with him. [29] But he replied to his father, "Look, I have been slaving many years for you, and I have never disobeyed your orders, yet you never gave me a young goat so I could celebrate with my friends. [30] But when this son of yours came, who has devoured your assets with prostitutes, you slaughtered the fattened calf for him." [31] "Son," he said to him, "you are always with me, and everything I have is yours. [32] But we had to celebrate and rejoice, because this brother of yours was dead and is alive again; he was lost and is found."

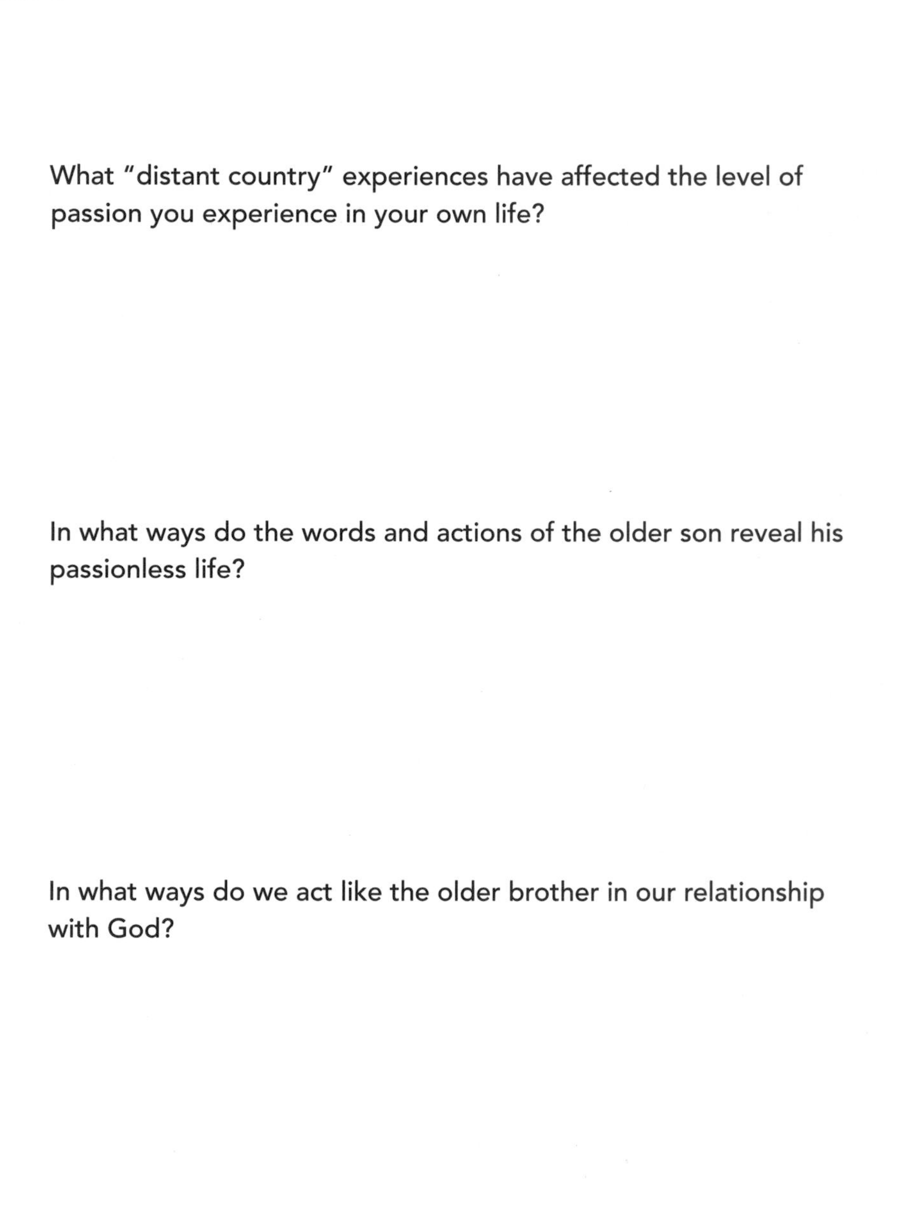

What "distant country" experiences have affected the level of passion you experience in your own life?

In what ways do the words and actions of the older son reveal his passionless life?

In what ways do we act like the older brother in our relationship with God?

The younger brother was self-centered and had rebellion in his heart. He perceived life with the father as dull, and his passion for life was misguided. The older brother perceived life with his father as duty, and his passionless approach to life made him miserable.

What is the danger of living on the fumes of passion and desire alone? What are the dangers of completely killing passion and desire?

At what point in life do you think most people lose their passion? What are some of the most common things that steal our passion for life?

Consider the possibility that your passion never really left you. It is a part of who you are at the very core, your truest self. But Satan will use anything he can—from distraction to defeat—to cause you to walk away from what it is that makes your heart beat strongest. Life is only once. Don't let the Enemy steal your opportunity to live fully, with passion and purpose.

Consider what really matters to you, what you care deeply about. How has Satan robbed you of your passion to live these things out?

WRAP

We were created with passion in our souls, but sometimes we have to fan the flames to rekindle the fire. That fire resides inside each of us, and Satan will try everything he can to put it out. God has placed eternity in our hearts. We were created with a desire to live for something greater, something bigger than ourselves. Our passion never really left us. It is a part of who we are at the very core, our truest self.

Remember these key thoughts from this week's study:

* God wants us to have the fire of passion in our lives.
* Something within us desires to live for something greater than ourselves.
* God wants us to have deep convictions because convictions are the foundation for the flame of passion.
* Misguided passion can leave you empty and lead you to a dead end.
* Passion for life is best when placed in the hands of God and His purposes.

DEVOTIONAL 1
AGAINST THE ODDS

GOD proves to be good to the man who passionately waits, to the woman who diligently seeks. It's a good thing to quietly hope, quietly hope for help from GOD. (Lamentations 3:25-26, The Message)

"Passion, intellect, moral activity—these three have never been satisfied in a woman. In this cold and oppressive conventional atmosphere, they cannot be satisfied."[1] —Florence Nightingale

The quote above reveals the world into which Florence Nightingale was born. Women were frowned upon if they considered any venture besides that of wife and mother, and certainly their passions were not encouraged. Today we remember Florence Nightingale as the mother of modern nursing. Because of her innovations, patients in her time enjoyed an unprecedented level of care. She believed that she had been called by God, and nursing was to remain her passion throughout life.

Many years passed between God's calling and Florence's response. For many of us, it's easy to act immediately when the calling is fresh and emotions run high. Passion burns bright, it burns hot, and sometimes, it burns quick. Florence Nightingale lived her entire life according to God's calling, according to her passion. As a result, she impacted the world.

How have you felt your passions constrained by culture or circumstances?

Imagine living your entire life dedicated to what you are most passionate about. There are no obstacles that are bigger than God.

1. Florence Nightingale in Hugh Grant's *Avenging Angel* (NY: St. Martin's Press, 2000), 11.

DEVOTIONAL 2
TRUE CALLING

"God is most glorified in us when we are most satisfied in Him." —John Piper[1]

"When I run, I feel the very pleasure of God."
—Eric Liddell, *Chariots of Fire,* 1981

Many are familiar with the story of Scottish Olympian Eric Liddell. Born into a family of missionaries, Eric was raised as a devout Christian. God was his first passion, but the Olympian was passionate about sports as well. He devoted himself in everything he did, including his love of sports, to the will and glory of God.

At the 1924 Olympics, Liddell refused to run in the 100-meter dash because it fell on a Sunday. Instead, he competed in the 400-meter dash which he was not favored to win. Eric not only won, but he set a new world record. Eric's ability to find God in a sporting event allowed him to experience both of his passions.

We can learn from Eric Liddell. We can glorify God in our everyday lives; we can feel His pleasure as we pursue our deepest passions. Your passion in this world and your place in God's kingdom may very well be two sides of the same coin.

What hobby, vocation, or field of study intrigues your heart in a serious way?

Spend some time in prayer this week. Ask God to show you where the Enemy has robbed you of your passion. Ask Him to reveal to you passions you may not even be aware of. Be still and listen.

1. John Piper, *Desiring God* (Colorado Springs, CO: Multnomah Books, 2011), 10.

DEVOTIONAL 3
EMBRACE THE DIFFICULT

"Passion is the degree of difficulty that we are willing to endure to accomplish the goal." —Louis Giglio

Then Jesus said to His disciples, "If anyone wants to come with Me, he must deny himself, take up his cross, and follow Me. (Matthew 16:24)

The last seven days of Jesus' life are known as Passion Week. During this week He was betrayed, beaten, spat upon, and deserted by His closest friends. Crowned with thorns and flogged, He was forced to drag the instrument of His own death to Golgotha, the hill where He would eventually be crucified.

We are called to take up our cross daily and follow Him, but do we know what that means? It doesn't mean to just suffer through a hardship in life. It means we sacrifice ourselves in that hardship and look for the purposes of God. It doesn't mean to just live with an illness. It means we abandon our will in favor of His. It doesn't mean we ask, "Why, God?" when things don't go our way. It means we ask, "What are you trying to teach me, God?"

What are you willing to endure to accomplish God's task for your life?

Trials and hardships will come—some of them more than you think you can bear. But what is a more worthy use of your passions than God's purposes? The next time you need to be inspired to stick it out through the more difficult, ask God to help you endure to the end. Ask Him to comfort you with His peace and joy.

LEADER GUIDE

HOW TO USE THIS STUDY

We're glad you've chosen to take your small group through *Stolen*. It is our prayer that this study will guide your group members into a discovery of the ways they can reclaim the treasures that God has set aside for them—their inheritance, strength, peace, dreams, joy, and passion. Before you get started, here is some helpful information about the different elements you'll encounter within the study as well as the resources you will find on the following pages.

Week Introduction: Each session begins with a narrative overview of the weekly topic. This material is designed to help you introduce the topic of study. You will probably want to read this before your group meets so that you'll better understand the topic and the context for your time together. For weeks 2-6, suggest that group members read this before you meet.

Flashback: This time is designed to provide group members with an opportunity to talk about what God has been revealing to them or what internal dialogue or conclusions have resulted from their devotion time during the past week.

Framing the Story: Your actual group time will most likely begin here with an icebreaker that is designed to help you ease into the study and get everyone talking. These questions are intended to be non-threatening to group members so that a pattern of participation can be established early on.

Reel Time: The first page of this section provides group members with a listening guide that gives them an opportunity to fill in the blanks on important points as they view the video message from Kerry and Chris Shook.

The second page is designed as follow-up to the video message. The bulleted items highlight the main teaching points from the video and can be used to process within the group what they heard and how they were affected. The discussion questions directly relate to the closing challenge in the video message and allow an opportunity for more personal application.

Small-Group Discussion: This portion of your weekly group meeting will guide group members to study passages that reinforce what Kerry and Chris teach in their video message. Each question is designed to lead the group deeper into the truth of the Scriptures they are studying and give them an opportunity to integrate these truths into their own lives.

Wrap: This section serves as a conclusion to the group time and summarizes key points from your small-group meeting each week.

Devotions: There are three devotions following each small-group session. These devotions will give group members an opportunity to take what they've learned during the session and continue the conversation in private devotional settings with God.

We hope the information we have provided on the following pages will better equip you to lead your study each week. In addition to the general notes to help you along the way, we have taken each question from the small-group discussion time and provided an explanation for why it is included as well as examples of possible responses when applicable. You will find this information on the DVD-ROM in your leader kit. Another item we've included on the following pages is a copy of the video listening guides for each session with answers. These may be useful to you if someone misses a session and would like to fill in the blanks.

SESSION 1
STOLEN INHERITANCE

Note: You may choose to bring your group together before your first "official" meeting to pass out member books, if you have purchased them in advance, or just to give folks an opportunity to check things out before they commit to participating in the study. This would be a great time to show the Study Overview segment (4:48) to those in attendance so they can get a feel for the content of the study as well as an introduction to the Shooks.

Week Introduction: Welcome group members to the *Stolen* study and make sure everyone has a member book. You may want to consider jumping to the Flashback session first this week and then come back to introduce the topic for Session 1.

Flashback: In weeks 2-6 this time will be used to talk about what God has been revealing to group members or what conclusions or internal dialogue have resulted from their devotion time during the week. In this session, however, you'll talk in more broad terms about their expectations and what most appealed to them about this study.

Framing the Story: Give everyone an opportunity to answer the first question. Then do the same for the second. Some members of your group will be more comfortable speaking aloud than others. Remember that the objective is to get everyone involved.

Reel Time: Play the video titled "Stolen Inheritance" (17:50). Encourage group members to follow along, fill in the blanks on page 10, and take additional notes as they hear things that speak strongly to their own stories.

Satan wants to:
steal your joy,
kill your dreams,
and destroy your relationships.

When you commit your life to Christ, you inherit all that comes with being a son or daughter of the King.

Satan tries to cover up the evidence of your inheritance.

We are complete in Christ; we lack nothing.

The evidence of your value is already complete in Christ.

After the group has viewed the video, direct their attention to page 11. Read through the Scripture passages at the top of the page as well as the main points from the video message that are bulleted below. You may choose to do this yourself or ask volunteers from the group to read portions aloud. This time is intended for discussion within the group about what they heard, how they were affected, and personal application. As time permits, allow group members to share other thoughts they had from the video.

Small-Group Discussion: In Session 1, you will look as a group at Psalm 8:3-5 and Jeremiah 17:9, contrasting how God created us in the beginning with what we have created for ourselves. You'll also look at Romans 8:15-17 and Ephesians 2:4-7 for more definitive illustrations of who we are in Christ and what our true inheritance is.

Check the DVD-ROM in your leader kit for possible answers to the group questions.

Wrap: At this point each week, you will want to close the group time in prayer. For this week, it's probably best for you to pray for the group. In coming weeks, as group members get more comfortable, consider asking for volunteers to lead the group in prayer.

Devotions: Encourage group members to complete the devotions before your next group meeting and remind them that you will be discussing what God has shown them through their time with Him.

Share that next week you'll explore how Satan attempts to steal our strength and how that can leave us exhausted physically and weak spiritually.

SESSION 2
STOLEN STRENGTH

Week Introduction: Welcome group members back. Use the narrative overview on page 21 to help you introduce the topic of study for Session 2. Make sure you read this before your group meets so that you'll better understand the topic and the context for your time together.

Flashback: This week you will be talking about what God has been revealing to group members regarding recovering their stolen inheritance. You'll also talk about ways group members were able to immerse themselves in God's Word and how that time better equipped them to move past any obstacles that were keeping them from reclaiming their inheritance.

Framing the Story: Give everyone an opportunity to answer the first question. Then do the same for the second. Continue to encourage all group members to share during this time.

Reel Time: Play the video titled "Stolen Strength" (18:00). Encourage group members to follow along, fill in the blanks on page 24, and take additional notes as they hear things that speak strongly to their own stories.

Change your focus from what you can't do to what God can do. (Joshua 1:6-9)

"So many times we focus on mountains that are in front of us — nothing is impossible with God."

Change your focus from your problem to God's power. (Joshua 1:9b)

Not all things are good, but God can bring good out of the worst things. (Joshua 1:13; Romans 8:28)

Speak in faith regardless of your circumstances. (Joshua 1:10-11)

Act in faith regardless of your feelings. (Joshua 3:15-16)

In the Christian life, God says, "You get in the back seat and pedal.

____

After the group has viewed the video, direct their attention to page 25. Read the Scripture passage at the top of the page as well as the main points from the video message that are bulleted below. You may choose to do this yourself or ask volunteers from the group to read portions aloud. This time is intended for discussion within the group about what they heard, how they were affected, and personal application. As time permits, allow group members to share other thoughts they had from the video.

Small-Group Discussion: In Session 2 you will look at Paul's description of his "thorn in the flesh" from 2 Corinthians 12:5-10 and the amazing transformation that took place in his heart. God promised Paul that His grace was sufficient. Using Paul's experiences as a framework, you will talk as a group about how Paul was able to find strength in God's promise, endure the difficult road he was called to, and how we can do the same in our lives.

Check the DVD-ROM in your leader kit for possible answers to the group questions.

Wrap: At this point each week, you will want to close the group time in prayer. This week you may consider asking for a volunteer to lead the group. Close out the prayer time, asking God to protect your group from fear, weakness, and anxiety and to help them trust instead in His power and strength.

Devotions: Remind and encourage group members to complete the devotions before your next group meeting.

Share that next week you'll explore how Satan attempts to steal our peace and how that peace is a valuable gift from God that can't be found in seeking after the things of this world.

SESSION 3
STOLEN PEACE

Week Introduction: Welcome group members back. Use the narrative overview on page 37 to help you introduce the topic of study for Session 3. Make sure you read this before your group meets so that you'll better understand the topic and the context for your time together.

Flashback: This week you will be talking about strategic decisions group members have made over the past week to operate in God's strength instead of their own. Encourage them to speak up about the progress they've made.

Framing the Story: Give everyone an opportunity to answer the first question. Then do the same for the second. Group members should be getting more comfortable with sharing by this point in your study.

Reel Time: Play the video titled "Stolen Peace" (16:45). Encourage group members to follow along, fill in the blanks on page 40, and take additional notes as they hear things that speak strongly to their own stories.

Counterfeits to peace:
We look for peace in our circumstances.
We look for peace in being comfortable.

If you're outside of God's will, you'll have no peace.

In the middle of God's will is the safest place we could be.

How do we reclaim our peace?
Trust in the security of God's priorities
Trust in the security of God's protection
Trust in the security of God's promises

After the group has viewed the video, direct their attention to page 41. Read the Scripture passages at the top of the page as well as the main points from the video message that are bulleted below. You may choose to do this yourself or ask volunteers from the group to read portions aloud. This time is intended for discussion within the group about what they heard, how they were affected, and personal application. As time permits, allow group members to share other thoughts they had from the video.

Small-Group Discussion: In Session 3 you will look at a couple of passages of Scripture that teach us what it means to find the hidden treasures of God no matter the circumstances in our lives. In 1 Peter 1:3-9, Peter talks about a "living hope" rather than how to minimize the dangers or eliminate the risks in life. In 1 Peter 4:12-14, you'll see Peter talk about rejoicing "as you share in the sufferings" and you'll have an opportunity as a group to talk about how that differs from denying our pain and suffering.

Check the DVD-ROM in your leader kit for possible answers to the group questions.

Wrap: Close in prayer, asking God to strengthen you even in the midst of your trials and to help you see the way He created for you to move forward through the turbulent waters.

Devotions: Remind and encourage group members to complete the devotions before your next group meeting.

Share that next week you'll explore how Satan attempts to steal our dreams by substituting counterfeits and how God never intended for us to underestimate the power of a dream or the power of pursuing a dream.

SESSION 4
STOLEN DREAMS

Week Introduction: Welcome group members back. Use the narrative overview on page 53 to help you introduce the topic of study for Session 4. Make sure you read this before your group meets so that you'll better understand the topic and the context for your time together.

Flashback: This week group members will have the opportunity to share victories they've experienced since the last time you met related to reclaiming their stolen peace. Everyone will have an opportunity to share changes they have made in their lives—mind, heart, commitments, relationships—to help them stay focused on God's peace.

Framing the Story: Give everyone an opportunity to answer the first question. Then do the same for the second.

Reel Time: Play the video titled "Stolen Dreams" (18:00). Encourage group members to follow along, fill in the blanks on page 56, and take additional notes as they hear things that speak strongly to their own stories.

The difference between dream and fantasy:
Dream includes all the bumps, bruises, and setbacks.
Fantasy is all fiction, no commitment, no work, no substance.

When we guard our hearts, it's also important that we don't lock our hearts down and kill our dreams.

One of the ways the Enemy paralyzes us is with fear.

Three fears that paralyze us from pursuing our dreams:
Fear of the unknown
Fear of criticism
Fear of failure

How do we know if a dream is from God?
It's bigger than our thinking.
It's unselfish.
It will match our gifts.
It will always align with God's divine plan.

After the group has viewed the video, direct their attention to page 57. Read the Scripture passages at the top of the page as well as the main points from the video message that are bulleted below. You may choose to do this yourself or ask volunteers from the group to read portions aloud. This time is intended for discussion within the group about what they heard, how they were affected, and personal application. As time permits, allow group members to share other thoughts they had from the video.

Small-Group Discussion: In Session 4 you will look at the story of the Shunammite woman in 2 Kings 4 and the dream she had allowed to die. You'll also look at the story of Peter walking on water in Matthew 14 and discuss as a group that sometimes it's not really about the dream itself —or even realizing the dream—but what we experience along the way. You'll also talk about the importance of keeping your heart alive.

Check the DVD-ROM in your leader kit for possible answers to the group questions.

Wrap: Request that a volunteer close your group time in prayer, asking God to help group members focus on not underestimating the power of pursuing the dream that God has placed in their hearts.

Devotions: Remind and encourage group members to complete the devotions before your next group meeting.

Share that next week you'll explore the difference in happiness and joy and how God never intended for us to live this life absent of joy —true joy.

SESSION 5
STOLEN JOY

Week Introduction: Welcome group members back. Use the narrative overview on page 69 to help you introduce the topic of study for Session 5. Make sure you read this before your group meets so that you'll better understand the topic and the context for your time together.

Flashback: This week group members will have the opportunity to share lost or stolen dreams that have been rekindled in their hearts and the plans they have for pursuing those dreams.

Framing the Story: Give everyone an opportunity to answer the first question. Then do the same for the second.

Reel Time: Play the video titled "Stolen Joy" (14:30). Encourage group members to follow along, fill in the blanks on page 72, and take additional notes as they hear things that speak strongly to their own stories.

Counterfeit to joy = happiness

True joy is deeper than our circumstances.

Joy isn't controlled by our circumstances.

Joy is a gift from God, but we have to claim it.

Joy goes deeper than our questions.

After the group has viewed the video, direct their attention to page 73. Read the Scripture passages at the top of the page as well as the main points from the video message that are bulleted below. You may choose to do this yourself or ask volunteers from the group to read portions aloud. This time is intended for discussion within the group about what they heard, how they were affected, and personal application. As time permits, allow group members to share other thoughts they had from the video.

Small-Group Discussion: In Session 5 you will look at John 9 and talk about Jesus healing the man who was blind from birth. You'll discuss how the man's blindness had a specific purpose—that God be known. And finally, you'll use Romans 5:2-5 to talk about our responsibility in changing how we see God in our circumstances rather than waiting for our circumstances to change.

Check the DVD-ROM in your leader kit for possible answers to the group questions.

Wrap: Close your group time in prayer, asking God to sustain you through your struggles so that you can ultimately experience true joy rather than seek after circumstantial happiness.

Devotions: Remind and encourage group members to complete the devotions before your next group meeting.

Share that next week you'll explore who actually gave you the gift of passion, how you can fan the flame to rekindle your passion, and how your passion reveals who you were created to be—your truest self. You'll also want to begin talking about what is next for your group when you complete your study of *Stolen*.

SESSION 6
STOLEN PASSION

Week Introduction: Welcome group members back. Use the narrative overview on page 83 to help you introduce the topic of study for Session 6. Make sure you read this before your group meets so that you'll better understand the topic and the context for your time together.

Flashback: This week group members will have the opportunity to share the false realities of happiness that they have been able to identify and destroy as well as specific truths that have enabled them to trust God more with their circumstances.

Framing the Story: Give everyone an opportunity to answer the first question. Then do the same for the second.

Reel Time: Play the video titled "Stolen Passion" (18:00). Encourage group members to fill in the blanks on page 86, and take additional notes as they hear things that speak strongly to their own stories.

Passion is the difference between fulfillment and frustration.

Passion is the difference between energy and fatigue.

When Satan steals our passion, he also steals our energy.

Passionate people change the world.

How we can reclaim our stolen passion:
Spend time alone with God. (1 Kings 17:3)
Decide not to ride the fence. (1 Kings 18:21)

Repair the altars in your life. (1 Kings 18:30)

Repentance always produces passion.

Live so that only God gets the glory. (1 Kings 18:37)

After the group has viewed the video, direct their attention to page 87. Read the Scripture passage at the top of the page as well as the main points from the video message that are bulleted below. You may choose to do this yourself or ask volunteers from the group to read portions aloud. This time is intended for discussion within the group about what they heard, how they were affected, and personal application. As time permits, allow group members to share other thoughts they had from the video.

Small-Group Discussion: In Session 6 you will look at how passion plays out in the story of the prodigal son—a passionate life for one son and his father and a passionless life for the other. You'll also talk about the dangers of living on the fumes of passion alone and the most common things that threaten to steal our passion for life.

Check the DVD-ROM in your leader kit for possible answers to the group questions.

Wrap: Ask as many group members as will to pray aloud, thanking God for this six-week journey you have just completed together. When all have prayed who wish to, close the prayer time praying that everyone will leave this study feeling empowered to live a passionate life.

ACKNOWLEDGEMENTS

VIDEO PRODUCTION TEAM

Producer: Rick Simms
Director/Script Writer: Bill Cox
Associate Producer: Betsy Wedekind
Lighting/Set Design: Steve Fralick
Equipment Manager: Aubrey Adcock
Video editing: Tim Cox
Graphics and Animation: Phil LeBeau and Tim Cox
DVD Authoring: David Watson

Teaching Session Production

Director: Rick Simms
Boom Camera Operator: Paul Lopez
Teleprompter: David Rogers
Camera: Aubrey Adcock
Makeup: Carol Frazier

Short Film Production

Director of Photography: Justin Wylie
Camera: Kyle Lollis
Audio Technician: Mike Psanos
Audio Boom : Clay Howard

CONCEPT AND EDITORIAL TEAM

Brian Daniel
Gena Rogers
Juliana Duncan
Bethany McShurley

ART DIRECTION

Jon Rodda
Christi Kearney

PHOTOGRAPHY

Micah Kandros

CAST

Josh Childs — John
Annie Kearney — Mary
Libby Spradlin — Ellen
Jeremy Childs — Thief
Jeff Durham—Detective
Greg Wilson—Mr. Greenwood

GROUP DIRECTORY

Name: ______________________________
Home Phone: ______________________________
Mobile Phone: ______________________________
E-mail: ______________________________
Social Networks(s): ______________________________

Name: ______________________________
Home Phone: ______________________________
Mobile Phone: ______________________________
E-mail: ______________________________
Social Networks(s): ______________________________

Name: ______________________________
Home Phone: ______________________________
Mobile Phone: ______________________________
E-mail: ______________________________
Social Networks(s): ______________________________

Name: ______________________________
Home Phone: ______________________________
Mobile Phone: ______________________________
E-mail: ______________________________
Social Networks(s): ______________________________

Name: ______________________________
Home Phone: ______________________________
Mobile Phone: ______________________________
E-mail: ______________________________
Social Networks(s): ______________________________

Name: ______________________________
Home Phone: ______________________________
Mobile Phone: ______________________________
E-mail: ______________________________
Social Networks(s): ______________________________

Name: ______________________________
Home Phone: ______________________________
Mobile Phone: ______________________________
E-mail: ______________________________
Social Networks(s): ______________________________

Name: ______________________________
Home Phone: ______________________________
Mobile Phone: ______________________________
E-mail: ______________________________
Social Networks(s): ______________________________

Name: ______________________________
Home Phone: ______________________________
Mobile Phone: ______________________________
E-mail: ______________________________
Social Networks(s): ______________________________

Name: ______________________________
Home Phone: ______________________________
Mobile Phone: ______________________________
E-mail: ______________________________
Social Networks(s): ______________________________

Name: ______________________________
Home Phone: ______________________________
Mobile Phone: ______________________________
E-mail: ______________________________
Social Networks(s): ______________________________

Name: ______________________________
Home Phone: ______________________________
Mobile Phone: ______________________________
E-mail: ______________________________
Social Networks(s): ______________________________